Ages

A Strange Journey

Susan Lavalle

Ages
Copyright © 2024 by Susan Lavalle

All rights reserved. No part of this publication may be reproduced, distributed, or transmitted in any form or by any means, including photocopying, recording, or other electronic or mechanical methods, without the prior written permission of the author, except in the case of brief quotations embodied in critical reviews and certain other non-commercial uses permitted by copyright law.

Tellwell Talent
www.tellwell.ca

ISBN
978-1-7-7962316-4 (Paperback)
978-1-7-7962317-1 (eBook)

Setting the Stage

When I was ten, the school nurse sent me home with a note to give my mother. It stated that I needed to have my immunizations updated—I was missing my last tetanus shot.

This made my mother aggravated and she instructed me to go into their bedroom and look through the bottom drawer of my father's dresser. There, she told me, I should find a copy of a letter from our family doctor, stating that I was highly allergic and could not have the last shot. I should get it for her.

While looking for this letter I came across something that shocked me, the shock of my life: a simple piece of paper that helped explain why I didn't quite fit in. It helped explain why I always felt as if I were a square peg being pounded into a round hole. Why I was always on the outside looking in. I just didn't fit. I was adopted!

I was almost three when it happened and had my full name changed. It went from Deborah Jane Henczenski to Susan Jean Van Brookhoven [now it is Susan Jean Lavalle]. I was adopted in an effort to save a damaged marriage.

After finding the papers I folded them up and stuck them in my pocket. Then I gave Mom the letter from the doctor she had wanted, and retreated to my bedroom. I copied the adoption papers, word for word. I had no idea why, but a small voice told me to do this and I did. I hid my copy and returned the original to my father's dresser drawer.

Now I understood why my mother seemed to always resent my very presence and why my older brother, Craig, seemed to hate me. I learned that she had lost a baby after having my older brother and she blamed Dad.

I also learned that, when they adopted me, she wanted another boy but Dad wanted a little girl. She gave in to his wishes, hoping to save the marriage.

Not long after I found the paperwork, Dad figured it out. He decided that we should sit down and tell me about it. When he said we would talk, you see, this meant to my father that *he* would do all the talking and *I* would listen. You were never allowed to question him, it was always "his way or the highway."

He told me that Craig had walked in one day to find his mom in the arms of another man. Once the war was over and the smoke had cleared, they had sat down and talked in an attempt to work things out.

Mom had explained how badly she wanted another child. As far as Dad was concerned, he would do whatever he had to keep his family together. He was a product of divorce and he didn't want this for Craig.

He explained that his parents divorced not long after they emigrated from Holland. He always hated having a different last name than his mother. Divorce was out of the question.

The father at their church directed them to an orphanage associated with the church. For those of you who are too young to know what this is, an orphanage was like a warehouse for children without families.

Dad told me that they had gone there a couple of times and left disappointed with the children the nuns paraded in front of them. They had agreed on a little girl, but Mom wanted a baby, maybe under one. Dad just wanted a girl.

They had gotten to a point where they were just about to give up. As they were leaving, Dad heard a garbage can fall over and heard someone yelling, "Get out of there, drop it, drop it!" He ran to see what was going on.

He watched as a dirty little girl crawled out of the can, holding a shabby doll missing a leg. Without saying anything to Mom, he turned to the nun and said, "That's her, she's the one."

I could never understand why he felt that had to share this with me. I already felt like I was a piece of trash. And now he had to tell me that they had fished me out of a garbage can. This only made me feel worse.

Neither one of them ever thought to tell Craig what they were planning on doing—they just walked in with a little girl in tow. He was six at the time, I was almost three. But instead of learning from Craig's reaction toward me they decided to try again.

So one day in September, they excitingly announced that they had to go someplace. They would be coming home with something special, *very special*, they said. We should behave ourselves while they were gone.

Left to our own imaginations, Craig thought he was finally getting that train set he had always been dreaming of and I thought that they were going to bring home a "pony." What little girl doesn't dream of having a pony?

You can just imagine how surprised we both were when they came home. Dad pulled into the driveway and immediately got out of the car with a diaper bag in his hands. He ran around and opened the car door for Mom. Out she came with a newborn baby boy in her arms and a huge smile on her face.

Craig was irritated. I don't think I ever saw him so angry. Instead of going over to see the newest member of the family, he turned and walked away. I was thrilled. I was, however, surprised, because they had nothing, absolutely nothing for him. No crib, no bottles, no car seat, nothing.

I can only imagine how Craig felt. For the first six years of his life he had had his parents all to himself. Then all of a sudden he was forced to share them with a little girl he saw as an interloper, and now, at thirteen, a baby boy, Gregory. Why? What were they thinking?

Now that Mom had the little boy she had always wanted so badly, her resentment toward me got worse. Not only was she verbally abusive, she started the hitting and slapping. She became physically abusive. She made sure that I fully understood that I was a burden—*her* burden.

One of her favorite phrases was "You own us," which quickly became "You owe me!" Something I could never understand, after all I never asked to be part of their family and a child never owes their parents anything more than their love and respect.

I could not understand what I had done to deserve this. Nor could I understand why my father didn't step in and stop her. After all, he was the one who wanted a girl. I had no one to help, no one I could turn to. No one at all!

Now, you need to understand that both of my parents were functioning alcoholics. They would go to work alright, sober, but as soon as they got home, the drinking would start. So what happened next should be no surprise.

Age of Sweet 16

A Year of Turmoil

I can remember the day as if it were yesterday. My sweet sixteen. Sitting at the kitchen table getting ready for school, mom placed a present in front of me.

My gift was wrapped in red wrapping paper, with a note written on the same paper that read: "We know you're going to do it, so you might as well do it at home." It had been nearly five years since the last time my parents had remembered my birthday and gotten me something. I was thrilled.

I eagerly unwrapped it. Surprisingly, it was a six pack of Miller beer. Beer. Now I had a license to drink and I quickly became the family bartender. They taught me how to make whisky sours, gin and tonics, all kinds of drinks. Now I had something in common with them. We all drank, including me.

Mom and Dad would drink from the time they got home from work until they went to bed. Craig and I would start as soon as we got home from school. As soon as I walked into the house, the drinking would start.

I would make myself a gin and tonic, more gin than tonic, in a twelve-ounce glass with three Oreo cookies. Then I would lie down on the living room floor with the music blaring. The only reason Gregory was not drinking yet was because he was only six at the time.

But at the tender age of six, he became my first angel. You heard me right. My *angel*. I have learned that, with time, God will use what or whoever He has at hand to find you when you are lost. And at that time I was lost, truly lost. So he used Gregory.

You see, our parents would often go out with their friends drinking. They would leave Craig and I home to babysit. As soon as they would leave, Craig would sneak out the back door, leaving me home alone with Gregory.

It was around this time that I found a Bible. I had never seen it open, had never seen anyone reading it. But something told me to put the book in my night stand, that someday I might need it. So I did. (To this day I still have that Bible with tape on the binding to hold it together.)

I found it to be a sanctuary. When my mother would get on one of her war paths and the screaming and hitting started, I would run to my bedroom. I would slam and lock the door behind me so she could not get to me, and would jump over the bed, pulling out the Bible from the night stand and throwing it on the bed.

Where it opened would be where I would start to read. I had no idea what I was reading, but I would read. Eventually, it would start settling me down. I had absolutely no idea what I was reading but it was giving me some peace.

However, I was still very depressed, and would often think about suicide. I was convinced that I was living in hell, so heaven had to be waiting for me right around the corner. All I had to do was to get the courage.

I would sit in my parents' bathroom with a razor blade just millimeters from my wrist. I would keep saying to myself, "Just do it. You can do it. Just think how bad they are going to feel every time they have to use this bathroom."

Then suddenly a clear small voice would call out, "Susan, I'm thirsty, can I have a drink?" I would put the razor down and get Gregory his drink. By the time I would manage to get him settled back in his bed the thought of killing myself would be gone.

This must have happened six or seven times before I realized that the Good Lord was trying to tell me something and I finally put the blade down for good. God had something planned for me; I just didn't know what.

It was around this time that two strange things happened. First, one morning, after a night of binging with the family, I woke up in bed, between my father and older brother. I had no idea what had happened, how I had gotten there, or if anything sexual had happened.

But after that my father started pulling me over the back of his chair, smiling, grabbing my ass, and saying, "You can do anything you put your mind to." Right in front of Mom, adding more fuel to the fire already burning in her toward me. I never understood why he would say or do this—or why *now*.

Craig also started to touch me in a way that made me feel very uncomfortable. While swimming in the pool he would swim under the water right up to me. He would then put his hands on the inside of my legs and slowly bring them up until they were in my crotch. Once he surfaced he would press his body against mine, without removing his hands, and whisper, "You need to shave your legs tonight."

Around this same time Craig started getting involved with drugs and one day I found his stash hidden in a teapot in the kitchen. I showed him what I had found and then called Dad to let him know. Craig got so angry with me he picked up a steak knife and threw it at me. The knife missed me by inches. I just stood there. I was frozen; I could not move.

Dad ran into the house and, seeing the knife sticking in the edge of the countertop next to me, told Craig to get out. Craig packed up and left, telling no one where he was going. He just left.

When Mom got home from work, Dad told her what had happened. He showed her the hole in the countertop and the bent steak knife he had pulled out of it. He showed her the drugs. None of this sank in; her only concern was where Craig had gone.

She blamed me for all of it and Dad just stood there in shock. For what I think was truly the first time, he began to understand how Mom felt about me.

After all of this I had a dream, a dream that convinced my mother that I was a witch. And I made the mistake of telling her. I told her that her father's nurse would call her in three days. She would ask her to bring my grandmother to the nursing home.

She would be asked to stay out in the hallway while my grandfather said his final goodbyes to my grandmother. Then he would close his eyes for the last time.

When this happened exactly as I told her, she announced to everyone that I was a witch, a *real* witch, and she stopped talking to me. After all, her eldest son was gone and her father was dead, and in her mind this was all my fault. Somehow I had caused all of this. She didn't even want to be in the same room with me.

It was during this time I stopped going to church. The church had failed me. I felt that my parents were hypocrites. I felt that they would go to church with all their fineries on to show off. Then they would come home, put their faith in a mason jar, and put it on a shelf over the front door. Only to grab it the following Sunday on their way to church.

I never saw them practice what they preached. If an activity didn't promise to make some money for them it was not worth doing. "Volunteering," to them, was a foreign idea, something they never did. Their idea of the golden rule was "He who has the gold makes the rules." So I stopped going to church.

But after an extremely difficult week, a lot of fighting, a lot of hitting and slapping, I agreed to go to church with them.

Don't ask me why. I hoped that this would help settle things down and she would stop the abuse for a little while. At least that is what I had hoped it would do.

I would go to church with them, but I would not sit with them. They always liked to sit in the middle, where everybody could see them. I decided to sit on the left side of the altar, about five rows back.

That's when it happened: my second angel. Directly in front of me sat a young mother with a little girl. The girl could not have been any more than five years old. She had long, blond curly pigtails flowing down her back. I watched as she would start to squirm and her mother would put her hand gently on her knee, lean over, and kiss her, to calm her down. She was very patient with her.

For some reason I just could not take my eyes off her. I could not stop staring at her. I knew for sure that she had to feel me staring; I just could not stop. I was staring so hard I thought I would burn a hole right through her.

That's when it happened. She turned and looked, with her bright, beautiful blue eyes, right at me and gave me a great big smile. One of those ear-to-ear smiles.

The whole room lit up—a bright, shining, blinding light covered the entire place. I could see nothing but the light. Then, just as suddenly, a wave of peace came over me. I had never felt such peace.

To this day I can't remember leaving the pew. All I can remember is that I walked out with such peace, I could not even feel the ground. I felt like I was walking on clouds. And the wonderful thing was, this lasted, this peace has stayed with me ever since (I am now seventy-one years old).

This bothered my mother so much that she would try extra hard to start fights. She wanted to see me cry. She wanted the abuse to continue, but she was in for a shock. About three weeks after the church experience, during a time when she was on one of her war paths, I finally got the strength and courage to stop it.

During the battle, while trying to escape to my bedroom, it happened. I stopped at the door. I caught my composure, wiped the tears from my eyes, and turned around. Shoulders up, I walked right back to her. Looking her straight in the eyes, I said, "You can hit me from here to hell and back again, I am never going to cry for you again."

The abuse stopped then and there. She never lifted another hand to me. Instead, she decided to continue not to talk to me altogether, which was fine with me—peace and quiet at last. I finally began to understand the very words I had been reading in the Bible. Now they started to make sense.

Now, as I look back to that year, a year full of turmoil, a year of depression and the desire to commit suicide, I see that God walked with me and brought me through it.

Since then I met and married a wonderful man, Robert. A man my mother felt was below her. I was marrying someone below their status. She would refer to him and his family as "white trash."

Her wedding toast to us was "I give you a year and you will be home with your tail between your legs, begging me to forgive you." This December first will be our fiftieth anniversary. Her toast only made me more determined to make my marriage work, just to prove her wrong. (Both of my brothers have been divorced twice since then.)

I have two great children and three strapping grandsons. That could only happen if I were here. I have earned two degrees and worked for twenty years with the physically and mentally handicap, and loved the work.

But life didn't always go smoothly. I did have two miscarriages and a number of car accidents, and have suffered a bankruptcy. But God walked with use throughout all of the turmoil as well as the blessings.

PS: If any of you are wondering what happened with the copied adoption papers, well, they came to good use. You see, one day while at a library, Robert found a small book that had the names, phone numbers, and addresses of the adoption agencies throughout America. I was able to write to the very agency responsible for my adoption.

If you ever decide to adopt, check your motive. If it isn't just because you have love—a lot of love—to give another person, don't adopt. Children don't ask to be part of a family—you are the one who makes the decision. So please, please, make sure your motive is LOVE!

I am sad to think that, to this day, Craig, at seventy-four, still sees Gregory and me as interlopers. To him we are still not family. Makes you wonder how long hate can last and why. I have forgiven him for how he feels but Gregory is still struggling with it. I keep both of them in my prayers.

Age of Twenty

The Proposal and a Sinking Boat

Before marrying Robert I had been dating a young man, Michael, who was an Annapolis candidate. We had talked about marriage, but for me, the dealbreaker was he "didn't want any children."

He felt the navy was no place to raise children. Robert, on the other hand, wanted children. He also accepted me just as I was; he didn't want or need for me to be something I wasn't. I know that I was not officer wife material. It would have been an unhappy situation for me.

I was the one to let Robert know that I was interested in getting to know him better. We worked at the same place; he worked in the photo department and I worked in the art department.

One day, during a break, I went and asked him how his bowling was and he told me that it was OK. It took one of his friends to tell him that I had just opened the door for him to ask me out. He encouraged Robert to ask me.

When it came to the opposite sex, Robert was a little shy, so, on our third date, he blurted out, "I don't know how, I don't know when, but I am going to marry you." This floored me. I accepted the proposal.

I came to the conclusion that I had to let Michael know that we didn't have a future. So one summer morning we went out on his boat so we could talk without any interference. He didn't seem to be too upset—I think he had come to the same conclusion and he didn't do or say anything to change my mind.

As we finished talking, Michael noticed that some bad weather was coming in and said we really needed to get back to the dock. I reminded him that he had promised me that he was going to teach me how to drive the boat. He turned the wheel over to me and showed me what I needed to do.

But as the bay was getting choppy he told me to floor it. We needed to go faster so we could get off the water before the storm hit, so I added some gas. That's when it happened. We hit something we didn't see and it took a layer of plywood off the bottom of the boat.

I looked down and noticed that we seemed to be taking on water and I told Michael as much. His response was that there was always water on the bottom of the boat, more so with wooden boats, and that I should just keep going.

As we continued heading for land, I looked at my feet again. The water was now a little above my ankle. I asked Michael about this and this time he acknowledged that we were taking on water. He immediately threw out the anchor, but he didn't shut off the engine. So there we were, zoom-zooming around and around, as the boat sank lower and lower in the water.

As I climbed up onto the deck to stay out of the water, he finally realized what was going on. He turned the engine off and then disconnected it. As I waved down another boat for help, he stood there with the engine over his head. He must have looked like a fool.

Some boater noticed us and they came to our rescue. After they helped me into their boat, they took the engine from Michael and began to scold him. They told him that his first concern should have been his passenger. He should have made sure I was safe. I should have had a life jacket. It upset them to think that Michael was more concerned about his engine than his passenger.

When I got home, I told my father everything that had happened. He rolled his eyes and said, "And he wants to drive a battleship." That was the last time I saw Michael.

Not too long after this I decided it was time for me to move out. So I began to gather furniture so I could furnish my own place. Mom didn't believe that I was really going to move out, so, thinking that she would prove her point, she took me to Ethan Allen to buy some furniture.

She know that if I didn't spend any money I was not going to make the move. I purchased three ladderback chairs. After fifty years we still have one of these chairs, which we use as a desk chair.

I started exclusively dating Robert in June. We moved in with each other in September. And on December first we got married. ALL in the same year (1974).

Most people who learn this are surprised to see that we have been married for nearly fifty years. And we are still going strong. We like to tease each other, saying that we are going to trade one of use for two half their age.

Then we laugh after one of us says to the other that we couldn't handle it. The other would say "Yes, but I would die with a smile on my face." But I wouldn't want to try to break someone new in. Robert is like a comfortable pair of old shoes, broken in just right

Age of Twenty-One

Moving to New Mexico

Robert and I spent our second Christmas as a married couple with his parents. We had decided to move. After a year of trying to get pregnant, our doctor suggested that we needed to get away.

He told us that the only reason he could think of that was preventing me from getting pregnant was stress. We had to get away from what was causing this stress. That meant getting away from my mother.

After eight parakeets, two guinea pigs (three by the time we arrived), and two dogs (Robert's effort to help get me out of my depression, after each time I thought I was pregnant and wasn't another pet would show up), Robert agreed to the move. He really didn't want to go, but he would. He knew how important this was to me.

We put everything we owned in his parents' basement, traded both our cars for a Jeep Cherokee, and packed up the animals, calling the Jeep "Noah's Ark." Three days after Christmas, we left.

With no money or job, off we went. We camped the entire way out, aiming for Roswell, New Mexico. Why New Mexico? My Great Uncle Clarence had spent a year, right after he returned from WWI, out there to play cowboy. As a child I spent hours listening to his stories and fell in love with the state. So, once we decided that we had to move, New Mexico seemed to be the perfect place.

The night before we entered the state we camped in the panhandle of Texas. Throughout the entire trip, Robert had our male dog, Columbus, sleeping with him in his sleeping bag. Columbus would curl up at Robert's feet and stay there throughout the entire night.

I, on the other hand, had Izy, our female dog. She insisted on sleeping in the fold of my sleeping bag. I had one of those bags with a nylon zipper and at least twice during the night, Izy would stretch her legs and out of the bag I would slide.

Our last night camping before entering New Mexico was so cold that we woke up with ice in the tent from our breath. We decided that we needed to stay in a hotel so we could warm up and get the tent dried out.

The next day, we had a chance to the see city. I didn't like it. It looked depressing, so we moved on, ending up in Albuquerque. We quickly found a small, not so nice efficiency apartment. Robert started his job hunt.

Our only income was his unemployment and food stamps. Every once in a while a care package from New Jersey would arrive, this always seemed to come when we really needed it.

Three weeks later, I got pregnant. We were thrilled; the move had worked. Finally, our family would grow. Somehow, I already knew that I was going to have a little girl, and I never questioned this—our Kathrine was on her way.

When Robert and I first got married we had sat down and written a list of names: two girls and two boys (Kathrine Joe-anne, Bethanne Joe-anne, Robert Paul, and Anthony William).

I can remember telling my parents that they were going to be grandparents. The first thing out of my father's mouth was "You can do that without a job?" I thought to myself, *You can do it without a marriage license.* How could such an intelligent man say such a stupid thing?

On the other hand, Robert's parents were thrilled they were going to be grandparents. They couldn't wait. Now his mother had an excuse to make baby blankets. (I still have a couple of them to this day, they are beautiful.) About a week later, Robert secured a job.

The first five months I had terrible morning sickness. I had a very hard time keeping anything down. Poor Robert, he always knew when I had gotten sick, especially on those days when I needed the Jeep.

He would come home from work to see a bucket with soapy water, paper towels, and cleaning fluid sitting in front of the car. He would not come in but set to work cleaning the Jeep. He knew that I couldn't clean it—it would only make me sicker, a bigger mess. He never complained.

As time got closer, I started telling him that I didn't want to bring our baby home to the apartment. Our landlord showed us a two-bedroom apartment she had available. But I just didn't want to bring our baby home to an apartment.

I wanted a home. Robert thought I was being silly. After all, we only had one income and no savings. He couldn't see how we would be able to do that. But I wanted a home, so he finally told me that, if I could find a house and figure out a way to pay for it, I should go for it.

So, I set to work. Kathrine would come home to our own home. I found a realtor who was willing to work with me. I explained our situation to her. She found a small one-bedroom home with an owner willing to hold the mortgage.

The monthly payment was about the same amount we were paying for rent. Now I had to come up with the down payment—$2,000. So Robert and I went to a car dealership and traded in the Jeep for an orange VW bug. We walked out with a car, owned straight out, and a check for $1,500. Robert then asked his father for the last $500 we needed.

I was thrilled. It wasn't much but it was ours. Kathrine would be coming home to our home. A home where we could start building memories.

Before Kathrine was born I had a number of false alarms. I would get up, wake Robert up, and then walk around the house until the contractions stopped. Robert had gotten used to this and he would simply roll back over and go back to sleep.

When I really was in labor he asked me if we could do it at a more reasonable time in the morning. Walking didn't stop the contractions, so I woke him up again, and told him that it was time.

When he finally realized that it was time, he got up, got dressed, and took me to the hospital. He called his parents to let them know it was time. They had come out so they could be there for the baby's arrival. Robert's father was thrilled. Kathrine was the first little girl born to the family in over forty years.

They had been getting a little worried, thinking they would miss it, that she would be born after they had to go back to New Jersey. Kathrine was almost two weeks late.

We were finally a family and the memories could start—memories like having her first Christmas with a tree that was so big we had to tie it to the curtain rod to keep it standing. Memories like Robert backing up to take a picture of Kathrine on her first birthday, right into her birthday cake. Memories like putting her in her stroller in the front yard with Columbus protecting her. Memories!

We had lived in this little home for about two years when we decided that it was time for Kathrine to have her own bedroom. So we started looking for a bigger home, and found one in Belen. Kathrine was all excited she would have her own room.

Before we actually moved into our new home, Robert and I spent some time getting Kathrine's room painted. We allowed her to pick the color of the walls—purple. After painting the walls, we put some corkboard up so she could stick things up. We painted the trim in her room a little lighter purple and she picked small doorknobs with roses on them for her closet.

The day came for us to actually move in. We started unloading the truck we had rented, putting everything in the den. Kathrine was so excited, she started jumping from one box to box.

It was getting late, time for her to go to bed. But she was too excited to settle down. All she wanted to do was to play, so she continued jumping from one box to another. We tried to get her to stop. We knew that she could get hurt, and that she really was getting tired.

Then it happened: she miscalculated a jump. She went down, hitting her nose on the hearth of the fireplace that was in the room. We picked her up, got a towel, and tried to get the bleeding to stop, but we couldn't.

We needed help. It was late and our phone had not been connected yet. We didn't know where the hospital was. So we went to the sheriff's station. One of their officers led us to the hospital.

Kathrine received a few stitches and was given some painkillers. When we got home she went to bed without any problems. I sat on the side of her bed and gently rubbed her shoulder until she fell asleep.

The next day, Robert went to work, and Kathrine helped me unpack. After a little while I could see that she was getting bored, it was time to do something fun. So we went for a walk; maybe we would meet some of our new neighbors.

Almost as soon as we started our walk we met a little girl, who would become Kathrine's best friend, and her mom. She lived two houses up from us. Kathrine immediately started playing with her—Lizzie.

I sat with Bertha, Lizzie's mother, while the children played. Kathrine was having a wonderful time playing with her newfound friend. I hated the idea that we needed to get to work. We had a lot of unpacking to do.

Bertha suggested that I leave Kathrine there so the girls could play. She said she would bring her home in a couple of hours so I could unpack without worrying. I called Kathrine over and asked her if she wanted to stay and play. She nodded her head yes and went right back to playing. The girls played for hours before Bertha brought her home.

The next morning got a little scary. I got up to start working on the unpacking, but I had to get Kathrine up, dressed, and fed. When I went into her room, she was not there.

I started panicking as I looked through the entire house. I was getting ready to call the sheriff when there came a knock on the front door. When I opened the door, there stood Bertha holding two little girls by their hands.

She told me that Kathrine had come to their house around 6 in the morning to play. I asked Bertha in for a cup of coffee. We both realized that Kathrine would do this again, so we came up with a plan.

I would pack her a little bag with her play clothes in it and put it by the front door. I would tell Kathrine to take the bag with her when she went to Lizzie's house. Bertha would feed both the girls breakfast and they would play.

Then Bertha would send both of the little girls back to my house around lunchtime. I would feed them lunch and then they would play at our house. This plan worked very well and continued until the children were old enough to start school.

Age of Twenty-Two

A Small Voice

While we were living in Belen we didn't have a car. We did everything, timed our shopping, and did all our travel using a scooter with a sidecar. Kathrine would sit on my lap in the sidecar as Robert drove.

We all had helmets to wear. But Kathrine had broken the strap on hers so she hadn't been wearing it. At this time I was pregnant with RT.

When we would go grocery shopping, Kathrine would sit on my lap on the way up. Once we were done shopping we would put Kathrine in the sidecar and pack the groceries around her. I had to sit behind Robert, which became a little scary since I was eight months along.

We always purchased two packages of Oreos. One package would be hidden away. It had become a routine. On the way home Kathrine would dig through the bags until she found one of the packages of cookies. By the time we would get home half of the bag would be gone and she would be covered with cookie crumbs.

One day something strange happened. While I was hanging up clothes in the back, a quiet, small voice came to me. It instructed me to fix Kathrine's helmet. I listened and did exactly what I was instructed to do.

The voice told me that it would come back tomorrow and that I should follow the instructions it would give me, without any questions. Robert saw me repairing the strap on Kathrine's helmet and asked me why. When I told him why he didn't question me.

The next day we went up to Albuquerque. We planned to watch the balloon parade and then get a new pair of shoes for Kathrine. The parade was wonderful, very colorful, and Kathrine loved it.

It was after the parade that things got a little scary. There was a lot of traffic; it was stop and go. Now, Robert had a bad habit when he rode the scooter. He would always look down at the oil gauge for some reason. This day, in stop-and-go traffic, this habit was a very bad one to have.

The voice returned. It instructed me to raise Kathrine over my head and to hold onto her as tightly as I could. So I did. Then Robert noticed that the flatbed truck had come to a stop.

He turned the wheel in an attempt to avoid the truck but it was too late. The sidecar slid under the end of the flatbed, only coming to a stop when my elbows hit the bumper.

The way Kathrine was sitting on my lap, if I had not followed the instructions given to me, she would have been decapitated. I thank the Good Lord that I listened to the voice and did as I was being told to do. Kathrine has grown up to be a wonderful woman, a wife, and mother of two handsome sons. She is a nurse with a big heart.

As the sidecar slid under the bed of the truck, I immediately gave my unborn son to God. I told Him that the baby belonged to Him and I trusted Him; the baby was in His hands. I was taken to the emergency room and both I and the baby were checked and were released with only a few stitches on my elbows. RT was OK.

It was at this time when my mother reared her ugly head in me. One day I was tired and Kathrine was fussing and nothing

I did seemed to settle her down. For some reason, I just didn't have the patience for her behavior. I was tired and very pregnant. I just could not handle this.

I quickly picked her up, holding her against the wall, shaking her. I started yelling at her. It was then, while looking at the tears in her eyes, that I saw my mother. I was behaving just like her—something I never wanted to do.

I slowly put her down and asked her to go to her room. I started praying to God, "Satan, get behind me." Once I had caught my composure, I went into Kathrine's room and sat down on her bed next to her. I apologized to her and promised her that I would never do anything like that again. With the Lord's help, I haven't.

Our son was born early, about a month early, and required some medical intervention. His name was supposed to be Robert Paul after his father, but Robert felt so guilty about the accident. He truly believed that he was responsible for all of the baby's problems.

So when he came to my hospital room, he told me that, under no circumstances could the baby be named after him. He didn't want the baby to grow up so stupid.

He then told me that he had picked out a name: "Tobias," which means "blessed by God." He didn't care what it was, the name could be Tobias Robert or Robert Tobias. I selected Robert Tobias (RT). It took a long time for Robert to work through his feelings of guilt.

I know that most people think that when you hear voices you are crazy. If that is the case, then I am happy to be crazy. I am here to say that this is not always the truth. We need to learn to listen, sometimes the voice is from God.

Age of Twenty-Six
Starting to Find the Missing Pieces

When I was almost twenty-six, Kathrine, RT, Robert, and I lived in the small town of Belen, New Mexico. We used to take short excursions to Albuquerque. We would go to their flea market or the public library.

One day while at the library, Robert found a little red book. It had all of the names, addresses, and telephone numbers of adoption agencies throughout the US.

He brought the book to me with it open to one of the pages. "Susan," he said, as he lay the book down in front of me. "Isn't that the agency who handled your adoption?"

I was a little surprised that he remembered the name. I quickly wrote down the information. Robert knew that this meant a writing spree was about to start.

It took me a little time to work up the courage to write the first letter, but with Robert's encouragement, I managed to compose my first letter. It had all the important information on it. The name, case number, and dates—everything I thought was important. I asked them to communicate with me. Now all I could do was wait and pray. A lot of praying.

It felt like forever, as I waited for some type of response. When it did come, I was extremely disappointed. The letter said that there was nothing they could do.

It went on to say that they could not give me any information on my birth parents—at least not until one of them contacted the agency. So I gave them my telephone number just in case.

A couple months later I received a call out of the blue. It was the social worker from the adoption agency. She informed me that she had just gotten off the phone with a member of my biological mother's side of the family looking for me.

They wanted to contact me but she needed my permission to give them my phone number. Without hesitation, I told her yes. Within a half hour I was on the phone with my Aunt Catherine, my mother's older sister.

She told me that they always wondered where I was and had hoped that I had a good childhood. She told me that my grandmother had asked her to find me and she had promised her that she would.

We talked for about a half hour before she asked me if she could give my grandmother my phone number. About a half hour later, I was talking to her.

We spoke for a long time but it only felt like minutes. I could not stop crying, I had so many questions. But the phone was no place to ask them, so we made plans for them to come out and visit us.

As soon as we got off the phone I called Robert. He could hear that I was crying and immediately asked if everything was alright. I shared with him what had just happened. My prayers had been answered. He knew how long I had been waiting for this moment.

I could hardly wait for them to visit. When the day finally arrived, I could barely hold back my excitement. Standing at the airport, with RT (Robert Tobias) in my arms and Robert holding Kathrine's hand, felt like an eternity.

It was strange. As soon as I saw Grandma Julia, I knew her. She walked like me, smiled like me, she even liked rubbing her fingers over different forms of textures, like newly opened paper. She even had us stop so she could walk barefoot in a small brook so she could feel the sand between her toes.

I watched as the pieces of the puzzle start to fall in place. I was seeing where the strange little things I loved to do came from. They had always wanted to find me.

During the visit, Grandma Julia explained to me that my mother, Deloris, had played a very important role in our finding each other. She told me that, one day while she was house cleaning, a picture of my mom fell to the floor. This wouldn't be so unusual except for the fact that the table the picture was on was across the room. She wasn't close to it; she didn't hit it.

So she went over and picked it up, put it back on the table, and returned to her cleaning, only to have the picture fall off the table again. This happened about three times before she got the idea and with this and stopped what she was doing and called Aunt Catherine.

She told her that she needed to find me. She gave Catherine everything she had about the adoption and the agency. With this in hand, Catherine called the agency. It was only after this call all the calling had started.

She told me that my parents were married and they seemed to be happy. She was not sure what had happened, but one day my father shot and killed my mother. I was eight months old at the time. She said that the police found my father sitting in his parents' kitchen; he didn't run, he just gave himself up.

The state presented my grandmother with two options when it came to me. They could either take me and adopt me or put me up for adoption. At the time they were not in the position to adopt me. Grandma Julia had an eleven-month-old baby and a husband dying of cancer at home. They just could not afford another child in the home.

The agency promised her that they would keep her updated about me. But they never did. I could see from her expression that it made her very angry. But she was even more angry when she learned about the abuse I had gone through at the hands of my adopted mother.

She kept apologizing to me. I kept trying to make her understand that this was not her fault, that she didn't have anything to apologize for. She had no way of knowing.

Now, Grandma Julia was a pleasantly plump woman and RT loved all the folds she had when she sat on the rocking chair. He loved crawling to her and putting on an act so she would pick him up. He would squirm a little to get comfortable in her folds. She would rock and sing to him as he fell asleep. He loved this.

One day, I asked her to take a close look at him. It was then that she realized that he had no tears in his eyes, that he'd been giving her crocodile tears. Laughing, she picked him up, kissed him, and said to him "You're a little actor." She gently rubbed his cheek, and gave him another kiss as he squirmed to get comfortable on her lap.

Aunt Catherine convinced herself that I had named our daughter, Kathrine, after her. She convinced herself that I had somehow remembered her when I was a baby. I didn't have the heart to tell her that this wasn't true, so I just allowed her to think this.

They spent two weeks with us and I loved every minute. I learned a lot; a lot of the missing puzzle pieces were coming together.

After they left I wrote a long letter to my adopted mother. I told her all about finding my biological mother's side of the family. I attempted to reassure her that I still saw her as my mother. I forgave her for everything. I can't tell you if she every accepted this. What I do know is that, by forgiving her, a very heavy weight was removed from my shoulders.

<u>**Truly forgiving others as the Good Lord forgave us is FREEING**</u>

Age of Twenty-Nine

Panic Big Time

Robert and I began to feel that we needed to do something for the Lord. We started looking for something, looking at the church bulletin board, hoping to find something that would tug at our hearts.

At first, we looked for something close to home, maybe something somewhere in New Mexico. But we could not find anything, so we broadened our search. We found a mission service in Denver, Colorado.

A church affiliated with our church was looking for a couple to manage a small apartment complex they ran. They were looking for a handyman and someone to run some small support groups.

We both felt that this was something we could do. So our church made arrangements for us to go up and stay for a weekend. Robert and I decided that we would make a vacation of it for all of the family.

We would go up, meet the church board, attend a Sunday service, and have a tour of the facility. Afterward on our way home we would stop and camp and have some fun.

At first everything went smoothly, right up to the end of the church service. RT, who was three, and Kathrine, at six, attended their Sunday school classes. I should have sensed something was going to go awry. RT had gone to the classroom without any problems.

RT was extremely shy and it was hard to get him to do anything new. He liked his routine, he needed to know what was coming next. He is still this way. So when he went to the class without hesitation I should have known something was going to happen; my mom radar should have sounded.

When church was over, everyone went to the cafeteria for a potluck and the children were let out of their classrooms to join us. Out ran Kathrine—she wanted to show us what she had worked on. But no RT.

I asked Kathrine if she had seen her little brother and she told me that she hadn't. That was when some panic started. RT was a little boy, small for his age. He had beautiful platinum blond hair and hazel eyes. He was a beautiful child.

The human brain can take you to places you really don't want to go. I started thinking that someone may have taken him. Had someone kidnapped him? Immediately, everyone started looking for him.

They searched the entire church building, along with all of the outer buildings. No RT. Some of the church members started walking up and down the street knocking on the doors, asking everyone they could if they had seen him. Still no RT.

The pastor called the police and they very quickly came. All I could do was cry and pray, so they had to speak to Robert. Robert showed him a picture of RT and told them what he was wearing.

Robert tried to calm me down but there was nothing he could do to help me. I just kept crying and praying. That's when one of the school teachers thought of something. She mentioned to the pastor that RT had made friends with another young boy in their class.

It was then that the pastor realized that that family was not there—they had left before all of the confusion. He called them and asked them if they had any idea where RT was. The father informed him that RT had come home with them. He'd told them he had permission.

The pastor told him that RT didn't have permission and he needed to bring him back to the church right away. As soon as their car pulled up and I saw my son I ran and grabbed him.

I gave him a great big hug. I could not let go, I just kept kissing him. RT kissed me back and then gently wiped the tears from my cheeks. The man apologized to Robert, telling him that RT had said he had permission to go with them.

Robert scolded him, asking him if it even dawned on him that maybe, just maybe, he should have asked us himself. After all, RT was only three. The man kept apologizing, put his head down and slowly walked to the car. Again he apologized and said he should have.

With that, Robert walked back to the pastor and thanked him and the rest of the church for looking for our son. Robert looked at me and saw Kathrine with her head on my shoulder, and me holding RT tightly. With that, he informed the pastor that we would not be taking the positions.

We packed up the car and headed home. We decided to camp on our way, in an effort to make the rest of the time fun. We stopped at a KOA about eighty miles from Denver. We set up the tent, had a cookout, ate dinner, and then went swimming in the pool.

But we were in for one more reminder that "Man plans but God wills." You see, as we were getting ready to leave, Robert realized that he had locked the keys in the car. The nearest locksmith was in Denver, eighty miles away, and even back in 1982, locksmiths were very expensive.

To say the least, we had to cut our vacation short. This was fine with me—I was more than ready to go home. Once home, we thought things would settle down, but!!!

The circus was in town and Robert's boss gave him some tickets to see it. We decided to go and make it an enjoyable time for the family. We would go to the circus and watch the shows and then go to McDonald's for dinner.

We would make a fun night of it. The children loved the acts. RT especially liked the clowns. On the way home, both Kathrine and RT fell asleep. We were all exhausted, but very happy, so we weren't ready for what happened next.

As soon as we got to the front door, Robert felt something was wrong. He held out his arm to stop us from entering the house. He told us to wait as he slowly entered the house.

He came back out and told us that we had been robbed, someone had broken in. He called the sheriff's office and reported what had happened. We sat outside on the front steps waiting for them to come and check the house.

We were only allowed in once the officers were done. They instructed us to write a list of what was missing. The thieves had gotten in by removing a window from a back door, which was strange since the door was unlocked the entire time.

They left all types of fingerprints. The officers could tell that the thieves were amateurs. We could tell this by what they stole. They took our dog, Cole, a bag of dog food, a can of rocks, and some jewelry. The jewelry was the only thing we were concerned about; as far as we were concerned, they could keep everything else.

We tried to make sure that our little ones didn't know what had happened. We didn't want them to be scared. We already felt violated and we didn't want them to feel like that. (Explaining why Cole wasn't home was easy since he had a habit of running away.)

The next morning, RT decided that he was going to give me a show—he was going to be a clown. Dressed in his favorite T-shirt, shorts, and the cowboy boots he always wore, he planned to try to balance on a ball.

While Robert was fixing the window the thieves had removed, I watched RT. Then it happened: RT let out a scream, Robert came running. The ball on which RT was trying to balance rolled out from under him and down he went.

We could tell that he had really hurt himself, but it was Sunday. Our family doctor wasn't in so we had to take him to the emergency room. They X-rayed him and found that he had broken his clavicle. But they didn't have a brace small enough for him, so they put one on that was a little too big on him.

They gave him some painkillers and instructed us to take him to our doctor as soon as we could. So the next morning, as soon as Dr. Brubaker opened his doors, we were there. I explained to him what had happened and he fit RT with a proper-fitting clavicle brace.

Being so young, RT healed quickly, which was great. School was right around the corner and I had registered him for a preschool program. Kathrine was thrilled about school starting—she loved school. I was hoping that going to a preschool would help RT make friends, help him to come out of his shell.

Kathrine and RT loved being read to. So every afternoon when it was time for their naps, we would sit on RT's bed and I would read to them. Kathrine had all the Dr. Suess books. Her favorite one was *One Fish, Two Fish, Red Fish, Blue Fish*. I can't count how many times I read this book to them.

Eventually, Kathrine started reciting each page as I read. At first I thought she had memorized the pages since I'd read this book so many times. But eventually she started saying the words before I had a chance to say them myself. So I decided to find out: was she really reading or did she just have the book memorized?

I got some index cards. On each card, I wrote one word of each sentence in the book. Then we sat down together at the kitchen table and I told her that we were going to play a game.

I held up one of the cards and asked her what it said. She had no problem telling me. Eventually, she started taking the cards and making her own sentences and then reading them to me.

Kathrine was reading, so when it was time for her to start kindergarten I informed her teacher of that. When they tested her reading, they informed use that she was already reading at the first grade level. I loved sitting on RT's bed and having her read to us.

Unfortunately, reading didn't come that easily for RT. I went around the house putting labels on everything. The hope was that he would begin to see that the word printed out was the name of the item. RT struggled with reading almost all his life.

For the first couple of weeks, things seemed to be going smoothly. Eventually, RT began to have issues with the school; he didn't want to go. I asked him what was going on and he showed me one of his papers and pointed to the picture. He told me that the teacher yelled at him because he couldn't color between the lines.

So I started looking for another preschool and found a lovely older woman who was running a small preschool in her home. RT warmed up to her right away. While we talked, RT went over and started playing with another little boy. RT would go there, starting two days a week and increasing the number of days as he was ready.

One day while both of the children were at school I received a call from the sheriff's office. They informed me that they thought they may have some of the things that had been stolen. They'd even caught one of the boys. Could I come down to ID the things?

I would be right down. Since we only had one car and Robert had taken it to work, I had to ride my bike to get to the station. So it would take me a little while. The officers said that this was fine and that they would keep the young man they had caught until I got there.

As soon as I arrived I was ushered into a room with a big table and chairs around it. There sat a young teenager, shaking, and his mother, who you could see was angry with him.

She looked at me crying. The officer asked me to sit down. Then he brought out a dirty sock. He turned the sock over and out fell our jewelry. "Are these yours?" the officer asked. I picked up my engagement ring and held it up.

As I was holding the ring I told them that this was the only thing that had hurt me. There was nothing else they took that had hurt so bad. The officers asked me if I wanted to press charges.

I took a good, hard look at the boy. He was crying and shaking. His mother was not much better, she was a wreck. I quietly slipped the ring onto my finger.

I told the officer I wasn't going to press charges. I then put my hand on the woman's hand. And I told both of them that I forgave them before I left the room. As I left I turned once more to take a look at them one last time. I could see a look of surprise and the young man laid his head on his mother's shoulder.

Finally all the trials were over, or so I thought. This had been a difficult year and at times I could not see the Lord. But I couldn't be so lucky. As soon as I got home I realized that I had locked all the doors and I'd forgotten my keys. I looked through the kitchen window and there they sat, right where I had left them. On the kitchen table. Now what?

I walked around the house looking for a way to get in. I checked all the doors. Everything was locked up; only the kitchen window was ajar. I would have to climb through that window.

I couldn't climb through the window without something to climb up on. The only thing I could find was my bike. So I secured the bike as close to the house as I could, then climbed up on its seat.

I carefully removed the screen and climbed through the window. (This was something I would keep to myself; if I told Robert it would quickly become a joke and I would never live it down.) I couldn't stop laughing when I thought to myself that the ring left through a window only to return through a window.

I couldn't help to think to myself that all of this was a sad situation. We had lived in a neighborhood where we thought we would never have to lock our doors. But because of the break-in, now we had to lock our doors. Maybe now things would get back to normal.

Age of Thirty-One

Fetch

After the panic in Denver, Robert and I began to think that maybe, just maybe, RT was ready to come out of his shell. Maybe he was ready to start making his own friends. RT always had to do things in his own time.

So we enrolled both of the children in soccer. I managed to get both of them on the same team, hoping that by seeing his older sister play the game he would get the idea and would get involved.

As shy as RT was, his sister was outgoing and making friends for her was very easy. Everyone who met Kathrine liked her almost immediately. It had always been extremely difficult for RT, but the friendships he did make were very close.

I agreed to be the team coach even though I didn't know anything about the game. One of the fathers agreed to be my assistant coach. He was asked to help teach the skills the children needed to know. The mothers were asked to bring the snack for our half-time. I asked them to bring something healthy, so they brought orange slices and water.

Watching the game was funny. It was like watching a beehive. Once the ball was in play the children would forget everything they were taught and all you could see were legs. You could not even see the ball, just children's legs. Just legs!

The only positions the children understood and did what they should do was goalie and guard. I made it my practice to rotate the children so each of them had a chance to play all the positions. My assistant and some of the more athletic children didn't like this but I felt that all the children should experience all the positions.

When it was RT's turn to play guard, he would stand there and look at the plants under him. He even ran off the field once to give me a flower he'd found under him. I thanked him for the dandelion and then asked him to return to his position.

But when he actually had the ball go through his feet, the time team got angry with him. So I pulled him off the field. He began to cry. He didn't like people being angry with him. He didn't understand why everyone was frustrated with him.

While he sat on the ground by the fence, a little brown dog came up to him and started licking his face. It was almost like the dog knew what he needed.

When I saw RT hugging the strange dog I went over to see what was going on. RT immediately asked me if we could take him home, if he could keep him. I told him we could but only if the dog followed us home. I was secretly hoping that its owner would show up.

But no luck. The dog followed us home, so now we had a new dog. RT named the dog Fetch and they became the best of friends. Wherever RT went the dog followed. He would sleep in RT's room and RT was given the responsibility of feeding him and keeping the yard clean after him. RT took on these chores with no fuss.

Age of Thirty-Three

A Move to New Jersey

One day I received a letter from Craig. This was extremely surprising since we hadn't had any communication for years.

He informed us that Mom was very sick; they thought she might have cancer. She was undergoing a lot of tests. He told me that we should at least know this, just in case.

I shared the letter with Robert and we decided that this may be the time for us to move back to New Jersey. The hope was that her illness had opened her eyes. Maybe this experience had taught her that family was more important than things—that was the hope.

We should have known better. But by the time we figured it out, I had already moved to New Jersey with the children. I moved first so I could get them in school, while Robert stayed in New Mexico. He was going to get the house closed up and try to get it sold. That was the plan.

I made an effort to make the move fun, to make it feel like we were on vacation. I had Kathrine look for Best Westerns for us to stay the night. Kathrine kept looking for ones that had a pool so we could play in the pool before bed.

When we finally arrived, Mom was there with the key to the Ship Bottom house. I foolishly thought that she would stay for a little while and start to get to know her grandchildren.

But I was wrong—about fifteen minutes later, some of her drinking buddies showed up. They were going golfing, so she left. Kathrine looked at me and asked why she didn't like them, asked why she wouldn't stay.

I struggled to figure out how to explain this to them. Both of them were upset with this. How do you tell small children the drinking and friends are much more important than family? I know that they didn't understand this.

I should have called Robert right there and then and told him that we would be coming back. But something stopped me. When we did talk about what had happened we decided that we would stay. At least his parents would have a chance to get to know their grandchildren.

At first things seem to be going smoothly. I managed to get Kathrine in her school without any issues. But when it came to RT, that was a whole other can of worms.

The school would not accept the paperwork I had brought with me from his school in New Mexico. They insisted that they had to do their own tests before they could put him in a class for special needs children. I found this funny. New Jersey's testing was only four pages long while the one from New Mexico was thirty pages.

Once he did get into the school he appeared to enjoy it. He seemed to like riding the school bus. But I began to notice a change. Instead of standing up tall and smiling, he began to appear depressed.

He seemed to be putting on a brave face when he was leaving for school in the morning. But that wasn't the little boy who got off the bus after school.

It took me little while to get him to open up to me to find out what was going on. Finally, he asked me if Robert and I were getting a divorce. I asked him where he had gotten this idea.

He said that most of the kids in his class only had one parent. They kept telling him that we were getting divorced and we hadn't told him. They didn't believe him when he would tell them that his daddy was coming, that he had both of his parents, a mommy and a daddy.

Once I got RT settled in bed that night I immediately called Robert. I told him that RT needed him. I told him about what was going on and that I really didn't care what he did with the house. RT needed him so he needed to get to New Jersey as soon as possible.

Robert assured me that he would do whatever he needed to do. He would be there as soon as he could. So with this, he made arrangements for a property manager so the home could be rented. This was supposed to pay the mortgage and the manager's fees.

He packed up a truck and headed out. We decided not to let RT know that he was on his way—we wanted to surprise him. As Robert was traveling he would call every night and speak to RT. RT was thrilled to hear from Daddy; this seemed to help him a little.

A few days went by and the children were in school when Robert finally pulled up. I wanted RT to be surprised. As Robert and I waited for his school bus to pull up, you could see him jumping around. The rest of the kids on the bus had no idea what was going on. RT kept yelling "Daddy, that's my daddy!" Getting off the bus he immediately ran into his father's arms.

RT didn't look back at the bus; he just wanted to stay in his father's arms. But I could see the faces of the children in the bus—they had smiles. Not long after that Kathrine's bus pulled up, and she saw RT hugging Robert. She ran to him and gave him a great big hug. Both of them got lost in his arms, crying. Neither of the children wanted to let him go.

When we planned our move to New Jersey, we decided that Fetch would stay with Robert in New Mexico. We explained to RT that Fetch would keep his daddy safe and when his daddy came to be with us, he would bring the dog.

RT liked the idea that his dog would keep his daddy safe. He would miss his best friend but Fetch had an important job. When Robert joined us he told us that he thought the dog was trying to gas him out. Boy, could he pass the gas. RT kept hugging Fetch and laughing while he listened to his father tell us about his trip.

But when my mother found out that we had a dog she started making things difficult for us. We weren't allowed to bring the dog into the house. He had to stay outside. RT couldn't understand this; after all, she had two great big dogs herself. *Why doesn't she like Fetch?* he'd ask. After all, she had never met him.

So, in an effort to keep her happy, we got Fetch a doghouse and chained him to it. RT would walk him when he got home from school. Play with him and feed him. He would police the area, all in an effort to keep my mother happy.

One time when we got back from the store, we found Fetch hanging over the neighbor's fence with only his back paws touching the ground. He had only been there for a little while, and Robert quickly helped him get down. We moved the house so he could not do that again.

But my mother still was not happy and she very quickly found something else to complain about: Robert's red VW. He had brought the VW Bug with him from New Mexico and it was sitting in the yard. His intention was to work on it. But Mom insisted that it had to go.

I knew it really hurt him, but he sold it. But even with that didn't stop her complaining—nothing we did made her happy. It was time for us to find someplace else to live.

We eventually found a home in Tuckerton, right on a canal. If we were able to put our canoe in the water, we would be able to use it more often. This was something everyone enjoyed, even Fetch.

One day while we were out on the water, some ducks caught Fetch's attention. Before we knew it, he'd jumped out of the canoe in an attempt to catch them.

It was only then that he seemed to realize what he had done. He quickly looked back at us as he landed, almost as if he was thinking that he had made a big mistake, in the water with a big splash. I never saw the dog move so quickly as he immediately turned around and swam right back to the boat.

Robert scooped him up out of the water. He was happy to be back in the canoe. This was his one and only time; he wasn't going to do that again. He did not even try to catch the ducks, even when they were in our backyard. Once was enough. I guess that the old saying "Look before you leap" fits perfectly here.

Once Again, "Man plans, GOD wills."

Age of Thirty-Eight

A Move to Florida

We had lived in New Jersey for about five years when once again the Good Lord started tugging at our hearts. We had found a wonderful church in the Germantown side of Philadelphia, and became quite involved. We enjoyed participating in their Living Nativity, and made a number of friends. On our way home from church we almost always stopped for hot pretzels—there was a man selling them just before you got to the bridge. Everyone loved them.

We started looking for a mission, a way to serve God. That was when we found a position in Sarasota, Florida. They were looking for house parents for children that had been abused, ranging from three to sixteen in age.

The home was owned by a Lutheran church and staffed by a Mennonite church. They flew us down for an interview and a tour of the home. Before we left they offered us the position and we accepted it. Once again, another move.

At first, things were going smoothly. Robert very quickly found a job and I got the children in school. Kathrine adjusted to her new school with no problems. They even accepted the paperwork from New Jersey saying she was gifted.

But things weren't that easy to get RT in the right classes, an issue the entire time he was in the public school system. I had brought with me the paperwork from his schools—about four pages from New Jersey and New Mexico's thirty pages' worth. They had to do their own testing.

Things seemed to be going smoothly. We established a daily routine and I would sit with some of the children, helping them with their homework, and tutor some of them. It even seemed that some of them liked helping in the kitchen, making dinner. They seemed to thrive when we gave them some responsibilities. We had even made arrangements for the children to go to the YMCA once a week.

But all this would change when a sixteen-year-old hurricane came to live in the house. She was a young lady with an extremely bad attitude. She had no control and when she became angry she would strike out violently, attacking whoever was closest to her.

We had attempted to let the church member we were supposed to report to know that she was dangerous, but they did nothing. They would not move her to a home more appropriate for her.

One day, the fat hit the fan. She got angry with a child half her size. She attempted to hit the young man. She started running after him. He locked himself in his room so she couldn't get to him.

Unable to get to the young man she started striking out at a child that was within hitting range, a little girl who was not even in their argument but was the closest to her. Robert had to come up from behind her and put her in a bear hug to restrain her.

Once things calmed down and the smoke cleared, she called the Department of Children and Family and claimed we had abused her. The DCF had to investigate the home and us. Once the investigation was over, they found the young lady's claim unfounded.

But they did find one big issue. The church that had hired us had failed to run a background check on us. We weren't supposed to start working at the home with the children until this was completed. This was a big no-no. The home immediately lost its certification. The DCF removed all the children from the home.

So, there we were, a little income and no place to live. But God didn't turn His back on us, He didn't forsake us. The Lutheran church, who owned the home, asked us to stay in the home until they could decide what they were going to do with it. They didn't want the house to sit empty. We would maintain the house and the yard for them, rent free. They were wonderful people to work with.

We started house hunting. While driving around, we came across a young man cleaning out a house. I don't know what made Robert stop, but he did. Maybe, just maybe, he was being moved by the Good Lord to stop. He asked the gentleman what he was going to be doing with the house.

The young man explained that he was preparing to get the house on the market. He said that his ex-wife owned the house and she didn't want to continue to rent it out. She had asked him to get the house ready to be sold.

We asked if we could go in and see the house. We both could see its potential. We asked him if we could purchase the home. He agreed to speak to his ex and see.

Once she agreed, they had a friend, a paralegal, prepare all the paperwork. We made arrangements for us to pay her monthly installments of the down payment, with a ten-year balloon payment. We assumed the mortgage.

Now, we had a house we could call home. Some thirty years later, we are still living in this house. A place where we started to build memories. Through it all we learned to cherish both the good and bad memories.

Age of Fifty

Finding my Father

A couple of years had gone by after Grandma Julia's death when Aunt Catherine finally asked me if I wanted to find my father. She'd had this information for some time but was afraid to share it with me because Grandma Julia had never gotten over what had happened.

She told me that she knew where he lived. She had known about this for some time. She knew that, when he got out of jail, he was still in New Jersey. She gave me his address.

I had been looking for him for a while. I even used the internet in my search. I found a John Henczenski. I had even called this individual but he told me that he was not old enough to be my father. I was very discouraged, only to later find out that he was my half-brother.

So I sat there for a while with the address staring at me. I was afraid to write. I kept thinking to myself, *What if he doesn't want to know me?* Robert kept telling me to write. He figured I didn't know him now so what would I lose if he didn't write me back? Robert has never understood how important it was to me to find the missing pieces of my life. I was scared that he would reject me.

Robert would have nothing to do with this. He kept trying to encourage me to write, and eventually talked me into it. So I wrote a long letter. I told him who I was, I told him that I would understand if he didn't want to write me back. Mailing it, I knew that I had to place this letter in God's hands; only time would tell.

It felt like years before I received a response. It came in the form of a package. All I knew was that it had my father's name and address on the envelope. I must have sat there for what seemed like hours simply looking at the package before I got the courage to open it.

When I finally did, I found it full of pictures, my original birth certificate, and other papers about the family. The letter he wrote told me that he had always wanted to know where I was, he had always wanted to find me.

But he was scared that I didn't want to know him. Everything that had happened, he said, was his fault. He was afraid I hated him. He wrote that when he got my letter he was afraid to write back. Would I be able to forgive him?

After the first letter we started a writing campaign. This continued until he finally agreed to come down and visit.

I can remember his arrival. Our daughter, who was pregnant with our second grandson, was with me when a red pickup truck stopped in front of our house. Kathrine and I just stood there, wondering who this man was.

We watched as he slowly climbed out of his truck. He sheepishly walked up our driveway. You could see that he was very nervous. At first, I just stood there, I couldn't move. I felt Kathrine touch my shoulder. I looked at her and smiled; that was all I needed.

I walked slowly toward him, then my pace quickened. I gave him a great big hug, and he started crying.

He had made arrangements to stay at a local hotel, but Robert and I would have nothing of this. We had rented a folding bed for us so he could use our bed during his stay. But he refused to put us out like that. He would sleep on the folding bed. So we agreed.

For the following week we spent as much time as we could together. I learned that he had spent six years in prison. He refused to tell me exactly what had happened.

All he could do was apologize, and you could see his posture change when I told him that I forgave him. This seemed to be what he had needed to hear. He could now be free from the prison of his own making.

I also learned that he had married three times and that I had a half-sister and a half-brother. I also learned that they had spent their summer vacations on Long Beach Island, an eighteen-mile island with a number of small towns on it.

They had stayed in Beach Heaven and he was surprised to learn that I had vacationed in Ship Bottom, a few miles away. I had even walked to Beach Heaven in order to buy some elephant ears (a fluffy pastry with cinnamon and sugar). I could have walked right past them and not even known it.

Lessons Learned

So what lessons did I learn through all of this?

1) We often hear people say "I found God." I think we have it backward. You see, I was not looking for Him; He came looking for me. I had all but given up on Him, and He found me. (Thank God He did.)
2) Don't shrug off the beggar on the street or that person sitting next to you on the bus—they may be the very angels God has sent to help and guide you. Treat everyone who crosses your path as an angel from God because you never know who is or who isn't.
3) Don't be discouraged. The Good Lord may find you today, but it may be years, or a lifetime, before you understand why. You may never know it at all. Just remember that He may use your simple smile, a hug, or a word of encouragement to another. You maybe someone else's angel.
4) Don't worry about what other people think of you, should you hear a still, small voice instructing you to do something; listen.
5) The Good Lord uses some strange thing to catch your attention.

6) Forgiving not only frees the individual forgiving but at times frees the one being forgiven. Sometimes, we build our own prison and forgiveness is the key needed to unlock the prison cell.
7) Trust the Good Lord—He will find a way for you. He even uses our mistakes for good, if we trust and believe He will.

www.ingramcontent.com/pod-product-compliance
Lightning Source LLC
LaVergne TN
LVHW042001060526
838200LV00041B/1815